Four Poets in a Boat

Four Poets in a Boat

An Anthology of Contemporary Japanese Tanka

Edited by Saeko Ogi
Translated by Saeko Ogi
and Amelia Fielden

Acknowledgements

Special thanks to Beverley George, who gave me professional and helpful advice, to Kay B., who helped me a great deal with her careful proofreading, to Amelia Fielden, who worked efficiently and cordially with me at translating, and to Noriko Tanaka, who inspired me at the stage of selecting poets for this anthology. Thanks also to Mari Uchida, my very dear granddaughter, who helped me to design the cover, using her computer skills to show me a variety of possibilities.

Four Poets in a Boat
ISBN 978 1 76041 631 7

Cover design by Saeko Ogi and Mari Uchida

First published 2018 by
GINNINDERRA PRESS
PO Box 3461 Port Adelaide 5015
www.ginninderrapress.com.au

Contents

Preface

Born in Tokyo, I have lived for forty-six years in Canberra. Perhaps it is an odd thing to tell you, but almost on the first day I arrived here, I began writing haiku and tanka in a notebook, even though I did not write them while I was in Japan. It was my way of keeping a diary.

Losing my husband in Tokyo in 1971 and coming here for the first time with my fourteen year-old daughter provided many occasions to look into my own life and into myself. I chose to write haiku and tanka, because they would express what I felt, simply and precisely. Of course my poems then were not written to show anyone else; my poetry diary was kept in a locked box.

I met Amelia Fielden way back in 1998. Since then, we have been working together, translating first, all types of poetry, and then concentrating on tanka. In 2000, I came to have contact with Inomata Shizuya, a tanka poet, and then I became a member of the Araragi-ha Tanka Society in Japan.

For some time, I have contemplated introducing contemporary Japanese tanka to poets writing tanka in English. I finally decided to publish an anthology of the work of four poets whom I met in Japan. They are all experienced tanka poets, especially Nagamori Satoshi, who started writing before 1964.

It is my pleasure and privilege to introduce you to this English-translated anthology of work by four Japanese poets, with a range of gender, age, interests and background, who nevertheless travel in the same tanka boat. I believe that you will share the poets' feelings and be inspired in many ways as you read on.

Saeko Ogi

Introduction

This book showcases the tanka of four contemporary Japanese poets. It emerges at a time when global interest in the genre is flourishing and it offers guidelines and inspiration by example for those who read and write this genre in English.

Its editor, Saeko Ogi, has selected the contributors carefully. The poetic voices of two men and two women of diverse ages, backgrounds and interests come together in unity but retain individuality. Their writing demonstrates just how effectively this diminutive genre can document our lives, address humanitarian concerns, and home in on the essence of all we experience or observe. When shared, they can promote harmony and understanding around the world.

The five-phase poetic genre originated in Heian times over a millennium ago and was known as waka, meaning Japanese song. It was only circa 1900 that the name was changed to tanka, meaning short song, thus indicating a willingness to share this brief but powerful genre with other nations.

The poet whose translated work appears first in the book, **Morigaki Takeshi**, is the youngest of the four. His teaching role extends beyond a professional, biotechnical one and encompasses participation in after-school clubs, including encouraging students to share their tanka with other national groups.

Humour pervades the writing but is grounded and relevant; wry not trivial. Teachers everywhere will recognise the following scenarios.

as if in a cage
of egg-laying hens
teachers
eat their lunches
in the staffroom

a female student
with an aristocratic face
nonchalantly
hands up a paper
as blank as fresh snow.

A serious tone shafts in, with skilful use of the tanka genre to address the essence of a contentious situation; not to make light of it but to come to terms with it. Morigaki Takeshi writes of his 'unfamiliar father' who has married for the third time and of his own struggle to acknowledge his new mother in respectful words that end up reading 'like an English text example'. This difficult circumstance is balanced by gentle references to domesticity and love of his own wife and child; celery soup on the stove, the sounds of his infant breastfeeding.

An enjoyable element of this sequence is the respect the poet holds for scientific fact, such as stem cell culture or the growth of bacteria in a white Petri dish. His fascination for science extends beyond the laboratory and addresses practical issues of agriculture and its future. It does not shrink from showing the sadder sides of farming such as the fate of cattle with diseased hooves which are 'taken somewhere far away'.

Robust and diversified, this sequence in which the poet sees himself as a 'gene boat' holds reader interest and offers an insight into a teaching philosophy that extends beyond the classroom and encourages curiosity and further learning.

I'm called 'leader'
but I stand
on the farm
neither as revolutionary
nor as liberator

The writings of the second poet, **Kuga Kumiko**, bring a change of style and subjects. Her poems indicate vulnerability and hint at a period of victimisation, but also demonstrate inner strength and a sense of staying true to herself; 'a woman who does not give in easily'.

Bird wings appear as a metaphor for desiring more from life:

> though I've been living
> just as I wish,
> behind my heart
> beating their wings ceaselessly
> birds still dwell

but seem to have found resolution in the mellow, final poem:

> the tranquillity
> of having no wings, perhaps –
> the days and months
> of a marriage
> pass by gently

The tanka in this sequence are imbued with honesty and self-knowledge as the poet tells herself, and us, truths of circumstance and struggle. But a sense of her own worth prevails in this significant and memorable poem:

> that ray of light
> beaming down from the sky
> today
> is a letter,
> a private letter to me

Kaku Hiroko, the third person in this poetic boat, demonstrates that tanka can deal with political reality. The irony of the tanka

while I listen
to the politician's boasting,
I polish
two go of rice
grown in Fukushima

extends to wide concern for others outside her home country:

saying 'take care'
the refugee family
waves goodbye
to the television reporter
and disappears into the darkness

Grief for the passing of her husband is shown in tender verses, in which she is unable yet to open his autobiography but strokes its cover; presses a leaf that once fluttered onto his back. Kaku Hiroko tackles the various negative aspects of ageing, including her own battle with diminished sight, with forthrightness and reality, but humour creeps in when she searches for vitamin supplements 'to oil an old bicycle'.

Gentler aspects of life find their place. A young man from whom she asks directions takes her hand and guides her there. Her mother's kindly nature is delightfully captured in just five lines:

my mother was the kind of person
who would break off a branch
of wintersweet blossoms
from her garden
for visitors to take away

As is the case for each poet in this book, the work of Kaku Hiroko merits rereading, not only once, but several times.

A love of the art forms of painting and poetry, linked to a philosophy of free thought and individualism, informs and enriches the tanka of **Nagamori Satoshi**. The fourth poet in the boat effectively combines these arts with a long-term sensibility for colours, fuelled in part by thirteen years' residency in France.

The fifty tanka gathered here are sourced from his collection *Cold Colours and Warm Colours* and span more than thirty years of his life. Throughout the selection, colours are named and described. Often they take on an active role as if they direct the painter's brush.

His sensitivity to nature on many levels permeates the tanka and yields such lines as 'wheat straw reflects the light'. Further examples include

> in the water are
> reflections from a row of poplars –
> wanting to paint
> these reflections, I wait
> for them to be disturbed

> treading on the frost
> in my garden, I go
> to scoop some water…
> water which flows, and
> water which wells up

The struggles and frustrations of achieving professional excellence are clearly delineated as the painter writes of 'unpaintable clouds', the 'spaces' that come into their own only later, and the necessity for the level of labour required to seem natural, not apparent. Occasional expressions of satisfaction with his own work are subtly expressed and bring a gentle smile to the reader.

Finally, a deeply satisfying tanka that summarises this poetic painter's commitment to his art:

as if discarding
impurities from my senses,
time after time
I throw away the water
from my brush-washing pot

The title *Four Poets in a Boat* brings to my mind's eye a coracle with a poet in each corner facing inwards. The voices are distinctively individual but the collection comes together as a harmonious entity. Careful editing and selection, combined with skilled translation, result in a book that makes a valuable contribution to contemporary tanka writing in English. This collection encourages individual poets as well as writing groups to explore ways in which they might expand and further develop their tanka-writing skills, while retaining deep respect for the genre's heritage and current practice in its originating country.

Beverley George
Founding Editor, *Eucalypt: A Tanka Journal*

Morigaki Takeshi

Born in 1982. After graduating from university, I started writing tanka with Kusunoki Seiei. Not long after that, I came to receive guidance from poet Tanaka Noriko.

2009: Received the twenty-third New Tanka Gendai Poet Award.

2010: Received the New Tanka Poet Award from Hyōgo-ken Kajin Club. Also nominated for the Gendai Tanka Collection Award.

2015: Annually joined in the Kyōto Jo-nan-gū Kyokusui Tanka Banquet to act the role of a Heian noble tanka poet with Kusunoki Seiei.

I teach biotechnology at an agricultural senior high school. Among the after-school clubs, I supervise the biology and literary clubs. In the former club, I lead the students to study locally rare creatures in Hyōgo through observation and research, and in the latter, I encourage the students to participate in submitting tanka to various tanka meetings nationwide.

The majority of my spare time, apart from working for the school, is spent exclusively looking after our baby. When I have a little spare time, I sow in the garden around our house seeds from fruit I have eaten. I dream of the day we can gaze at a growing orchard, when our child is older.

Qualified as horticultural decorator grade 3.

50 Tanka by Morigaki Takeshi

from *The Gene Boat* (Gendai-tanka Sha, 2016)

when I spread
the still moist manure
immediately
there's a smell
of flourishing earth

I have to work
even on public holidays
. . .
wordlessly
I'm turning over the earth

deep in the night
of a new moon
cucumber sprouts
pushing up through the ground
like zombies

bees visited
the male flowers
on the cucumbers –
the flowers will shortly
finish their work

cultivating
the newborn morning light
each night
you must put it in a glass
and drink

what a sad life
jellyfish have,
swimming around
as vaguely as
the recollection of first love

it appears that
the shadows of flowers
fallen on the ground
in August,
are more human-like than I

today again they say
'the hottest summer ever',
so I'm considering
fleeing from the heat
down into the land of roots

when I look up
I see, all over the sky,
a school
of silvery fish
about to pass by

a new term:
dolphins swim in my brain
from morning onwards
I'm engaged
in exam preparations

I'm called 'leader'
but I stand
on the farm
neither as revolutionary
nor as liberator

in an experiment
to measure its salinity,
I scoop up seawater
on a night as black
as leopard flower seeds

while the radiance
of the full moon
bathes my back
I pour a culture fluid
into a beaker

on the moon
that floats across a deep black
expanse of sky,
echo the sounds
of the mythical maiden's footsteps

a female student
with an aristocratic face
nonchalantly
hands up a report
as blank as fresh snow

this is most likely
the jawbone
of a whale:
death spread out
on the desk-top

cattle
with diseased hooves
put in a vehicle
and taken somewhere
far away

to the question
'will there be a tomorrow
for agriculture?'
the green caterpillar
just returns silence

as if in a cage
of egg-laying hens
teachers
eat their lunches
in the staff-room

tomatoes
cast away into a hole
in the paddy field
are still breathing
faintly, even now

like a catfish
glaring
under a huger than usual moon,
I hide myself
in the alleyway

an old faucet
in the bachelor hostel,
not turned right off
leaks steadily, sounding
like the underground railway

your back
clad in a coat
is departing
with the expressway
as its 'borrowed landscape'

in my fading memory
there is always
apple fragrance
about the person
of my lover

it was as if
I'd been told
'you're a descendant
from the race which
could not board the Ark'

this traffic jam,
it's like crabs
on the seashore
clustered together
making busy sounds

burying my head
in a down jacket
and squinting
to withstand the wind,
I must wait for you

passing clouds –
dendrobium orchids bloom,
and my wife
informs me of the results
of her medical examination

my wife crosses
through the lens
of the water droplets
on the green leaves
of the taro plants

on the far side
of the door
to the old family home,
my unfamiliar father
has his own space

‘today I
paid my respects
to my new mother’ –
I write that down
like an English text example

on the roof
of my father who’s marrying
his third wife,
a chilly rain
is falling…

it must be
some base sequence error –
or else
the birth of a new species,
this remarriage

with the nucleus
of my cells
remaining silent,
this loathsome day also
will come soon to an end

when I stand up,
aware of the hardness
of this wooden chair,
the world appears
to expand just a little

the kitchen is filled
with the fresh scent
of celery
as I wait for you at night
cooking our soup

as if they want to say
the individual and the whole
are the same,
light flashes from the scales
of a school of sardines

in the darkening
eastern sky
of clump of clouds –
spreading now
is a colony of mould

I am culturing
stem cells
in a liquid
the colour
of cosmos flowers

in a laboratory dish
are spreading bacteria
as white
as a sandy beach
bathed in winter sun

as I listen to the sound
of rain dripping,
the transplantation
of stem cells in the pipette
is completed

from the east
a red moon emerged –
that moon is one
which has left the system
and stands alone

today, too, as dusk falls
I steep
in the bath tub
this body called
'a gene boat'

dark matter
appeared on the black screen
where the pulse
of a white foetus
is beating

high in the sky
was the eclipsed moon
when fertilised eggs
were implanted
deep in my wife's womb

he could have been born
as a species of bird –
I touch
the birth hair
on my child's back

in his hand
that is about the size
of a tulip bulb,
there is a seed to be grown
eventually into a giant tree

oh great winds
of mid-winter, blow not
on my child
who knows nothing
of the freezing cold

words that are not
in any dictionary,
day by day increasing –
my child converses
with the remnants of crumbling snow

while I'm baking
apples which are called
'the wisdom fruit',
I'm listening to the sounds
of my child breastfeeding

Kuga Kumiko

In my childhood, I was an unhealthy crybaby, which must have annoyed my mother. About the time when I went to school, I was a miserable child, withdrawn and fragile. For some family reason we moved to Nara to live.

I cannot forget the scenery of the Nara countryside that I saw then for the first time more than half a century ago. The paddy fields were filled with thick, prolific, rice ears, framed by the scarlet cluster amaryllis covering the footpaths. On the field banks bloomed gentians, dianthus, even golden lace, which we see now only in the flower shops. I tossed my school bag onto the ground and ran about in the field until dark. I forgot then that I was vulnerable health-wise.

That scene is not there any more. Villages have become big towns. Many streets have been laid out. Changes still continue. I live here quietly watching these alterations.

50 Tanka by Kuga Kumiko
from *Sketches of Time* (Anbisha Bunko, 2015)

1. Junction

from 'Junction'

swallows
with spring madness in their breasts
sail smoothly
over the street
again and again and again

such a strange being,
the one I call 'father' –
inside his body
a grain of wheat
that has not sprouted

the junction
at which a clear stream
becomes a muddy flow –
impossible to gauge
the human heart

'A Change of Occupation Is Announced'

don't touch him,
the one with big-boned arms
exposed,
who is wielding a pan
in front of the fire

he says
'no regrets at all,'
but, ah – I am
simply a seagull
flapping about in dismay

pointing at
the crooked face of the woman
in Picasso's painting,
he said with a serious look
'that's you, there'

you are a woman
who does not give up easily,
his eyes tell me
as swish, swish, swish
I wash the white cabbage

being carried along
in the rough current
a leaf of a tree
from the outset
has no words to say

hey you
who are lost in thought:
secretly
I have been in love
with three men

this trivial matter
resembling the lightness
of a lily,
brushed my fingers
with a chilly touch

using
a sharp razor blade
I shave your cheeks
and your guilty conscience
both at the same time

if you say
life is one long journey,
whereabouts
do the falling flower petals
conceal you?

when I think
of my life which has passed
blamelessly,
I feel loneliness sharp enough
to pierce the sky

from 'Deep in the Mountains'

when I touch
a bunch of still-green grapes,
I have the feeling
of life itself pulsing
against my fingers

I become a traveller
to an ancient world,
walking mountain paths
as I beat my way
through the rough grass

that ray of light
beaming down from the sky
today
is a letter,
a private letter to me

from 'A Tanka Workshop'

'we'll meet again' –
in the twilight
after the workshop
each of us is a warrior
wounded all over

to you
standing there stronger
than a new-leafed elm,
I spoke no empty words
and then we parted

from 'Flower Names'

my youth past,
I'm watching the performance
of dolphins
who are no longer able
to return to the ocean

from 'Crossing the Overpass'

there is also
a way of life like
flying into the midst
of the thunderheads
which block one's passage

from 'An Autumn Woman'

the chrysanthemums
I've arranged are heavy
with perfume –
my mother must be here,
back from Hades

from 'Lingering Sunlight'

surely they are
more lonely than we of this world
are lonely –
yet perhaps the dead
might reply they are happy

from 'A Spring Flower Garden'

as I suppress
my hopeless feelings,
a gentleness of rain
is falling silently
on the spring fields

chanting 'me, me'
all together
Chinese chives bloom
and stretch high
their long thin necks

2. Thousand Lights, a Thousand Mice

from 'Evening Dreams'

shutting both eyes
I listen to the sound
of my blood flow
pulsing ceaselessly
deep in my ears

my grandmother,
who had gone blind,
comes in a dream
and shouts at me
to light the lamp

waking from a nightmare
I brush with my fingers
the husband
who lies beside me –
just to check his warmth

from 'The Cucumber Spoke'

the person
whom I can never
see again,
has left two wheel tracks
on the surface of the road

in the cucumber patch
a cucumber spoke, saying
I want to bend
as much as possible
and try to live on

from ‘The Child’s Voice’

from the blooms
on the quince tree
wet with drizzle,
scarlet water is dripping
at the height of spring

such intensity
possessed by cherry blossoms
blooming in profusion –
have I ever
asserted myself?

from 'Becoming Single'

the warmth
of his fingers touching me
without words –
so deeply in love
with him, once

I added
just a pinch of salt
thinking
sometimes lies too
can be a subtle seasoning

from 'A Thousand Lanterns, a Thousand Mice'

that day when
filled with rage I hit him,
I return home
bearing on my back
the whole night sky

how it resembles
a broken heart,
this ripe tomato
slightly staining
my white chopping board

now how many dead
are there – in the town
I look down on
from the heights, I see
a thousand lanterns lit

from ‘There is One Wound’

returned
to the Other World, my mother
comes in my dreams
saying something to me
that I cannot hear

from ‘The Night Moon’

loving him,
hating him, forgetting him –
frankly, it’s a relief
to curl up in my bedding
and go to sleep

3. One Person's Shadow

from 'One Person's Shadow'

recollections
of wounding, of being wounded,
with the passing of time
soften as water does
in the sunshine

from 'Snow Falls'

what is the sky
angry about now, I wonder
gazing upwards –
such a large volume of snow
to fall in spring

4. Sketches of Time

from ‘The Indigo-coloured Mug’

I’m living here
with just a small crack
opened for the evil
within my heart
to inhabit

from ‘The First Prayer’

in general
I waver alone,
I decide alone –
the regrets and pains
all belong to me

from ‘Under the Lamplight’

there are no poems
about your lonely feelings
of childlessness,
says my husband one night
under the lamplight

though I’ve been living
just as I wish,
behind my heart
beating their wings ceaselessly
birds still dwell

from 'The Chipped Tea Bowl'

once more I realise
that words bear both
a true meaning
and a superficial meaning:
'I'd like to see you again'

from 'The Maze'

between permitting
and forgetting
I often
lose my way
on the dark moors

human life
forever a maze –
deep in my desk drawer
I find there is
a little desert

From 'As Few As Cherries'

my husband says,
using the past tense,
'you were kind
and you didn't complain' –
does he mean me?

From 'Under the Plum Tree'

since the day
I gave this abandoned cat
the name
of Putin, Russia
has been close to me

From 'Sketches of Time'

the tranquillity
of having no wings, perhaps –
the days and months
of a marriage
pass by gently

Kaku Hiroko

Member of Neiraku Tanka Group and Araragi-ha Group.

Perhaps the tanka collection of Ishikawa Takuboku was my first encounter with tanka, in my teens. I was so impressed that only thirty-one syllables could convey feelings as freely and expressively as this poet does. This is not what ordinary people can do… Since then I have read collections of other poets who have become popular topics of conversation, and also submitted my tanka to various places. Sometimes I even manage to gain an honourable mention.

In those days I happened to meet again, after some fifty years, my teacher Mr Inomata Shizuo, who was a Man-Yō-Shū scholar and tanka poet. He invited me to write tanka, offering kind guidance in his tanka group. He often told us that 'Tanka is the proof of your life and a confession of your emotions.'

At present I am losing my sight gradually, suffering from age-related retinal degeneration. However, I enjoy writing tanka supported by clever technology and my generous tanka friends.

50 Tanka by Kaku Hiroko
from the Araragi-ha Society's Journal, 2014–2016

The year 2014

borne on the wind
the sounds of temple bells
echo through the evening
as the shiso flowers
spill and scatter

while I listen
to the politician's boasting
I polish
two gō* of rice
grown in Fukushima

taking in my hand
my husband's autobiography,
I stroke its cover –
still this heartache
stays with me

* gō: a quantitative measure; one gō=180ml

'please give me
a little more time' –
I can't open
the autobiography
of my deceased husband

not knowing how ill she was,
I, her son's bride,
failed
to make allowances
for my irritable mother-in-law

taking a detour
to buy sake
for his father-in-law,
my young husband comes home
on a misty moonlit night

smoothly stripping away
Earth's thin skin,
I pluck weeds
from the garden
on a fine May day

in my garden
bloomed the flowers
of a Tongan pumpkin
from seeds scattered
last year at the winter solstice

in my memory, now,
I'm watching a B29 bomber
heading north
as the moon was rising
above the Bungo channel

The year 2015

the train departs
snatching away kindergarten kids
for their outing –
from under the vending machine
come loud insect sounds

as I age
my gums have shrunk –
I apply lipstick
to my mouth
as if I'm grieving

three years ago too
I was waiting
in a faintly creaking
treatment chair
for the second generation dentist

above the chimneys
of an abandoned factory
hangs the day moon,
whiter still
than pampas grass ears

the friend
who came to visit
shouldering a bag of new rice,
also brought along
a ladybug

the letter I sent my husband
before we were married,
has ended up
in the box for letters
belonging to my mother-in-law

at the end
of long hours of tests,
going straight home
with opened pupils
is hazardous

without waiting for
my pupils to contract,
I leave the ophthalmologist's –
the bright spring light
is really piercing

do people pass away,
I wonder, abandoning
idle thoughts
of this world, and
with their pupils wide open

my mother was the kind of person
who would break off a branch
of wintersweet blossoms
from her garden
for visitors to take away

a fallen flower,
blown by the wind,
flutters
onto the back
of my terminally ill husband

that fallen flower
which rested
on my husband's back
is pressed now
between the pages of my diary

I search
through the advertisements
seeing if there are
any vitamin supplements
'to oil an old bicycle'

when I ask the way
of a young man in jeans
with ripped knees,
he takes my hand
to lead me there

using the Chinese chives
budding in my plant pot
as a cushion
the stray mother cat
is suckling her kittens

no sign of the nursing mother
who was there till last night –
the Chinese chives
are still flowering, but
the she-cat has disappeared

the cicadas' voices
have suddenly ceased –
ten in the morning
in the silent town where
the temperature is 30 degrees

hearing on the news
that this country is first in the world
for longevity,
I made up my mind
to rebuild my home

their teacher, who
strongly advised my older brother
and others
not to enter a military academy,
has died in jail

The year 2016

I, who could never
ever, let my children go,
watch
the Syrian mothers
and pull myself together

saying 'take care',
the refugee family
waves goodbye
to the television reporter
and disappears into the darkness

leaving behind
a whispered 'we're going ahead',
the fallen leaves
went fluttering across
at the red traffic signal

anti-nuclear messages
stuck up there at the time
of each nuclear test,
leave no space on the inner walls
of the atomic bomb museum

I remember well
my mother-in-law saying
in the bright moonlight
of the second month,
'your gentleness does not appeal to me'

when I pull the thread
called 'memory'
sunk deep within me
a red camellia
comes floating up

in the rosy sky
is a spider's web
spread out
like an exquisite piece
of lace work

are the cherry blossoms
in full bloom
issuing an invitation?
my friend begins telling me
her innermost thoughts

opening grandfather's diary
I wake from their sleep
the silverfish
which have dwelt there
for 150 years

apparently silverfish
do not care for ink –
they breathe
between the lines
without eating the words

several years
since grandfather's room
was opened up –
in the stagnant air
silverfish are squirming

stories donated
to the local museum
have started to disappear, too –
the pile of old books there
a heavenly mountain for silverfish

in the village house
where no one has resided
in a long time
silverfish draw breath
clandestinely

leaving unused
some of the customary
eau de cologne
I gave him for Father's Day
my husband departed this life

beyond love and hate
a seductive wind arose –
voices
of the leaders of Japan and USA
at Hiroshima

in early summer
coming to Hiroshima
to preach
a path to peace, leaders
who know nothing of the War

in Hiroshima
the wind rustles green leaves
in new-leafed trees,
all of them, all
younger than I

human beings
fight and reconcile
over and over,
meanwhile military weapons
grow ever more powerful

I will not forget
the Atomic Dome –
though it slants
the Dome still stands
dominating all around it

on the small fan
I made by hand,
ten goldfish,
each with a smile
in its black eyes

lured by thunder
goldfish are dropping
all around me,
so realistically
in my siesta dream

each time I wave it
the goldfish on my fan
increase in number,
and around my body
leave images of swimming

Nagamori Satoshi

Born in 1928, I will be 89 years old this May (2017). In my youth I had a dream of becoming a painter. I have realised this dream and have become a professional artist. I have held my individual exhibitions fifteen times in all sorts of places in Japan, mainly in Tokyo and Osaka. Also I have never missed joining in the Annual Shunyō-kai group exhibitions. Colours are my great pleasure, which is perhaps innate. I am known as a colourist amongst artists.

I lived for thirteen years in France and have a great love for the life and art of the country. I still miss my over six years spent in a small village in the Bourgogne region.

Among many painters I particularly admire Odilon Redon's sensibility of colours. Painting should not be only descriptive reality. Neither should be tanka.

My late wife, Nagamori Mitsuyo spent her life protesting against the Araragi way of tanka. I understand her. I had, as well submitted my tanka to the Araragi tanka group until its end. Now I am a member of the Araragi-ha, a much smaller group, and write tanka more freely. There are not many tanka collections by painters. I have a collection, called *Cold Colours and Warm Colours*.

At present I am wheelchair-bound. I lead a solo life in the facility of a small village in Shinshū highland. I would like to sustain my own fantasies to express in my painting and tanka.

50 Tanka by Nagamori Satoshi

from *Cold Colours and Warm Colours* (Gendai-tanka Sha, 2013)

France 1964–1967

from 'Sacré Coeur'

Sacré Coeur
its hill-top steeple milky-white
when the sun shines,
and now purple
as the shadows fall

from 'The Skinned Rabbit'

when I saunter
down the stairs
I see
in the neighbour's garden
a skinned rabbit

from 'Father's Passing'

that day
I was contemplating
the gushing spring
at Mt Volvic –
was that when Father died?

from 'The Light at Ten in the Morning'

over numerous houseboats
come echoing
Christmas bells
from the church
on the shore

from 'Loophole'

the smell
of the onions
stings my eyes –
for what purpose am I
staying in this country?

France 1965–1967

from 'Gladiators of Old'

I, being accustomed
to resting
on green grass,
am puzzled
by Spain's terracotta soil

From 'She Who Returns Home'

what should I,
whom she is encouraging,
say to her –
she is leaving Paris now
in a taxi

Japan 1967–1971

from 'Vermeer'

from the bottle she holds
she is pouring
a stream of milk –
that is what
makes this painting

France 1971–1978

from 'Père-Lachaise Cemetery'

in front of the jet-black
unadorned tomb
of Delacroix
there is one tranquil
pot of chrysanthemums

from 'Venice'

I buy roast sweet potatoes,
then go along the streets
of Venice – maybe
my wife, who's ill on this trip,
will eat some

from 'Swiss Travels' 1973

when I walk the woods
in the freezing fog
hoar frost drips on me –
the woods are white, the sky is blue,
today is Christmas Day

from 'Oh, My Doll'

swallows are flying
poplars flutter their leaves
wheat straw reflects the light –
I so want to see
my ailing mother

Japan 1978–1979

from 'The Bellflower'

scarlet cloud-trails
are disappearing
from the sky…
now comes the blue
of Mt Yatsugatake at eventide

from 'The Radiance of Beyond' 1980

treading on the frost
in my garden, I go
to scoop some water…
water which flows, and
water which wells up

from 'The Knife Blade'

for several days
the snow around my studio
shows clearly
where rabbits have been
and pheasants have passed

from ‘Cubic Snow’

the snow exists
virtually in cubic form,
and this existence
is what possesses
the town of Takada

After 1986

from ‘Revisiting Bourgogne’

in the water are
reflections from a row of poplars –
wanting to paint
these reflections, I wait
for them to be disturbed

from ‘The Model and the Student’ 1989

without exception
the beauty of her form in repose –
I was gazing
at the model
during our rest period

from ‘Anemone’

with the passage of time
from blue twilight
to black night
the white highland lilies
shone radiantly

from ‘The Crimson Chintz’

as if discarding
impurities from my senses,
time after time
I throw away the water
from my brush-washing pot

from ‘The Trembling of My Senses’

just occasionally
the gods have gifted me
with ability
in tonal harmony.
but I don’t tell anyone

what was it
that I could not obtain
though I tried so hard?
what was it
already lacking at my birth?

from ‘The Day of Our Silver Wedding’

my wife’s heart
roams to its content, turning
in directions
where my heart
never goes

from 'The Blue of the Mediterranean Sea'

I rejoice
in the colours of southern France:
they harmonize
with the sense of colour
I've had since birth

from 'The Blessings of the Louvre, the Blessings of Paris'

I ponder
the blessings of Paris:
every day
of my seven years in Paris
I've learnt self-reliance

from 'Disappointment Hope Disappointment'

the beauty of the colour tone
created on my palette
today
does not transfer as it is
onto the canvas

from ‘Reds Which Illuminate Each Other’

lying dormant
in my sensory being
are the feelings
which were nurtured
during my thirteen years in France

from ‘The Deer’s Paw-prints’

was there a fawn
among the herd?
in the mud
around the forest spring
are paw-prints

from ‘The Tactile Feeling of Existence’

trying to deepen
my powers of observation
I focus on myself
until observation
connects with expression

from 'My Wife's Gaze (1)'

some days
in the atelier, I can feel
from the next room
my wife's gaze…
that invisible gaze

from 'The Fireplace'

seated beside me
when she was alive
Akiko would watch
flames burning in the fireplace,
burning as they still do now

from 'The Tip of a Short Blade'

two kinds of shapes:
those that are vanishing,
those that are appearing –
in the depths of the shapes
lies an existence

it's as if
the paints aligned
on my palette
have their own voices –
this morning, the red voice

from 'My Wife's Gaze (2)'

the lemon yellow
has a greenish tinge,
and looks subdued
when placed underneath
the warm yellow of sunflowers

the efforts of seeing
the efforts of considering
the efforts of drawing –
none of these accumulated efforts
must be apparent in your work

from 'Things Which Cold Colours Bring'

colder, colder –
today too
everyone is telling me
to increase the cold colours
in my paintings

though I lose my way
among the tones
of cold and warm colours,
my mind is clearing
with the purity of cold colours

from ‘Things That Are Unpaintable

I was watching clouds
being born,
one after another –
how can I paint
the unpaintable?

from ‘Homeless’

asking for no goods,
asking for no money,
yet staying alive –
tell us about this mystery,
someone who is homeless

from ‘Free Sky’

in paintings, the sky
should be the most free
for interpretation –
yet I can’t paint this free sky
as freely as I wish

from 'The Pure Grey Colour'

believing that
space which says nothing
will some day
come to say something,
I continue painting

from 'Winter in a Mountain Villa'

reddish-yellow needles
fall from the conifers
forming thick piles
and softly swelling
the paths on the high plain

from 'A Distant Red'

the time has come
for Yatsugatake to be covered
completely in red –
its prominent red peaks
control the whole of red

from 'Pictures I Have Not Finished Painting'

can I paint
my heart, as it moves
with the brightness
the darkness, the stillness,
the fierceness – of clouds?

from 'New Red'

I can say
I have matured
painting pictures –
when secretly
I wish that

that red
I am looking at now
is the red I saw
when I was young –
and yet it is a new red

people say
'break down one wall' –
however
there are visible walls
and invisible walls

intending
to throw away the old key
that in the end
does not fit the keyhole,
I have kept it for years

from ‘The Large Yellow Tree’

in a deep-sleep dream
I am walking along,
walking along a corridor
carpeted on and on
with inexhaustible red

from ‘Munch’s Darkness’

is it a human shadow
is it a spread of black hair?
I feel menaced
by this darkness
in Munch’s canvas

List of Original Tanka In Japanese

原歌リスト

Morigaki Takeshi　森垣　岳

「遺伝子の舟」現代短歌社（2016）よりの五十首

when I spread ... 湿り気の残る堆肥を一斉にまけば華やぐ大地の匂い
I have to work ... 休日も勤務日となる「・・・」無言で土をかき混ぜている
deep in the night ... 新月の夜更けに土をかき分けてゾンビのごとき胡瓜の発芽
bees visited ... ミツバチがキュウリの花を訪れぬ　やがて役目を終える雄花に
cultivating ... 産みたての朝の光を培養し夜毎グラスに入れて飲むべし
what a sad life ... 初恋の記憶のごとく曖昧に泳ぐクラゲのかなしき日々ぞ
it appears that ... 八月の地面に落ちた花影が我より人間らしく思える
today again they say ... 今日もまた「一番暑い夏」なので
根の国へ避暑を考えている
when I look up ... 見上げれば空一面に銀色の魚の群れが過ぎ行くところ
a new term: ... 脳内にイルカの泳ぐ新学期　朝から試験の準備しており
I'm called 'leader' ... 指導者と呼ばれてますが革命も解放もせず農場に立つ
in an experiment ... 塩分の定量実験するためにぬばたまの夜の海水を汲む
while the radiance ... 満月の光を背後に浴びながら培養液をビーカーに取る
on the moon ... 黒々と拡がる天上浮かびおる月に
嫦娥（じょうが）の足音ひびく
a female student ... 高貴なる顔の女生徒平然と新雪白きレポートを出す
this is most likely ... これはおそらく鯨の顎の骨でしょう
机の上に死が広がりぬ
cattle ... 足病みの牛は車に乗せられてどこか遠くへ連れられて行く
to the question ... 農業に明日はあるかという問いに芋虫はただ黙秘で返す
as if in cage ... 採卵鶏のケージのごとし教師らが職員室に昼飯を喰う
tomatoes ... 田の穴に捨てられているトマトらは今もかすかに息をしている
like a catfish ... いつもより巨大な月に睨まれてなまずのように路地に隠れる
an old faucet ... 独身寮の古き蛇口は完全に締まらずメトロの音を漏らせり
your back ... コート着た君の背中は去ってゆく高速道路を借景として
in my fading memory ... 薄れゆく記憶の中の恋人の姿はいつも林檎の香り
it was as if ... 箱舟に乗れぬ種族の末裔がおまえであると言われたようだ
this traffic jam, ... 賑やかな音立てながら群れている磯辺の蟹のごとき渋滞
burying my head ... ダウンジャケットに首をうずめて目を細め
風に耐えつつ君を待つべし
passing clouds – ... 行く雲や白きデンドロビウム咲き妻は診断結果を告げる
my wife crosses ... 里芋の青き葉のうえ水滴のレンズの中を妻が横切る
on the far side ... ふるさとの家の扉の向こうには見知らぬ父の空間がある
"today I ... 「私は今日、新しい母に挨拶した」英語の例文みたいに記す
on the roof ...三人目の妻を娶れる我が父の屋根に冷たき雨が降りつつ
it must be ... 塩基配列のエラーもしくは新しき種の誕生としての再婚
with the nucleus ... 細胞の核は無言のままにして
忌むべき今日ももうすぐ終わる

when I stand up, ... 木の椅子の硬さ気になり立つ時に
世界はわずかに広がり見ゆる
the kitchen is filled ... キッチンにセルリの青き匂いして
君を待つ夜にスープを煮ており
as if they want to say ... 個と全は同じであると言いたげに鰯の群れの鱗の光
in the darkening ... 暮れてゆく東の空の雲の群れ　広がってゆく菌のコロニー
I am culturing ... 秋桜の花の色した溶液に幹細胞を育んでおり
in a laboratory dish ... 冬日さす砂浜白き色をした菌の拡がるシャーレー一枚
as I listen to the sound ... 雨垂れの音聞きながらピペットで
幹細胞の移植を終える
from the east ... 東より赤き月出ぬ　あの月は組織を離れ独り立つもの
today, too, as dusk falls ... 遺伝子の舟と呼ばれし肉体を
今日も日暮れて湯船に浸す
dark matter ... ダークマター黒き画面に現れし白き胎児が脈を打ちおり
high in the sky ... 月蝕の月高々と受精卵胎内深く妻に宿りぬ
he could have been born ... 鳥類に産まれることもできたのだ
我が子の背なの産毛に触れる
in his hand ... チュリップの球根ほどの手の中にやがて巨木となるための種子
oh great winds ... 大いなる真冬の風よ凍りつく寒さを知らぬ我が子に吹くな
words that are not ... 辞書になき言葉が日毎に増えゆきて
ちぎれて残る 雲と語る子
while I'm baking ... 知恵の実と呼ばれし林檎を焼きながら
子が乳を飲む音を聞きをり

Kuga Kumiko　久我　久美子

歌集「時の点描」あんびしゃ文庫（2014）よりの五十首

①　分岐点

「分岐点」より

swallows ... つばくらめ春の狂気を懐に
街をいく度もすいすい過（よぎ）る
such a strange being, ... 父といふ未知なるものよ体内に
発芽せざりし麦のひと粒
the junction ... 清流が濁流となる分岐点　人のこころを計りかねゐる

「転職を告げらる」より

don't touch him, ... 骨太の腕をさらして火の前に
鍋を振りゐる君に触るるな
he says ... 悔いなんぞないと言ふ人ああ我が
ただおろおろと一羽のかもめ
pointing at ... ピカソの絵の歪んだ女の顔を指し
おまへがゐると真顔に言へり
you are a woman ... あきらめの悪い女と目で言はれざぶざぶざぶと白菜洗ふ
being carried along ... 激流に流されてゆく一枚の
木の葉もとより言葉をもたず

hey you ... ねえ貴方がなにかに夢中でゐる内に
わたしは三人（みたり）の男に恋した
this trivial matter ... ひんやりと指に触れたる白百合の
重さにも似てたわいなきこと
using ... 剃刀のするどき刃もてその頬と君のやましさもろともに剃る
if you say ... 一生を旅と言ふならどのあたり降る花びらは君を隠せり
when I think ... あやまたず過ぎこし生と思ふとき空突きぬくるやうな寂しさ

「山深く」より

when I touch ... まだ青き葡萄の房に触るるとき命が指を打つ気配する
I become a traveller ... 遠き世の旅人となり荒草を打ち払ひつつ山路を歩む
that ray of light ... ひとすぢのひかり空より降りくるは
けふ一通の我への私信

「合評会」より

“we'll meet again” – ... 「また会はう」合評会の夕暮れは
誰もが満身創痍の戦士
to you ... 新緑の楡よりつよく佇つ君に儚きことは言はで別れき

「花の名を」より

my youth past, ... 青春は過ぎてしまへりもう海へ
帰れぬイルカの芸を見てゐる

「陸橋わたる」より

there is also ... 立ち塞がる入道雲の真ん中へ飛び込むやうな生き方もある

「秋の女」より

the chrysanthemums ... たつぷりと挿したる菊の香り立ち
黄泉より母の帰りてをらむ

「暮れなづむ」より

surely they are ... 寂しかる現し身よりも寂しからん
否（いいや）楽しと死者ら応へむ

「春の花園」より

as I suppress ... 叶はざる思ひ鎮めて春の野に音もなく降る雨のやさしさ
chanting “me, me” ... 細ながき首を差し伸べいつせいに
わたしわたしと花韮の咲く

② 千の灯千の鼠

「夕べの夢」より

shutting both eyes ... 両の目をつむりて聞ける耳底を
打ちて止まざる血流のおと
my grandmother, ... 盲目となりたる祖母が夢にきて
明かりを点けよとおらぶ声する
waking from a nightmare ... 指触れて確かめてをり悪夢より
覚めて傍 への夫の温みを

「胡瓜が言へり」より

the person ... ふたたびをまみゆることのなき人が路上に残しし轍ふたすぢ
in the cucumber patch ... 思ひきり曲がって生きてみたかると
胡瓜が言へり胡瓜畑に

「みどり児の声」より

from the blooms ... 濡れそぼつ木瓜の花よりくれなゐの
水したたりて春まつさかり
such intensity ... 咲き盛る花の烈しさかくばかり主張せしこと我にあつたか

「一人になるとも」より

the warmth ... 言葉なく触れくる指の温かさ一途に人を恋ひし日のあり
I added ... ひとつまみの塩をはらりと加へたり嘘もときには良き隠し味

「千の灯千の鼠」より

that day when ... 渾身の怒りに人を打ちし日は夜空ぜんぶを背負ひて帰る
how it resembles ... 壊れたる心にも似て熟れトマト白まな板をうすらに汚す
now how many dead ... 今そこに死は幾つある高みより
見下ろす街に千の灯ともる

「傷ひとつある」より

returned ... 幽世（かくりよ）へ帰りし母の夢に出で
もの言ひくるも声の聞こえず

「月の夜」より

loving him, ... 人恋ひて人を憎みて人忘れさばさばと夜具にくるまりて寝る

③　影法師ひとり

「影法師ひとり」より

recollections … 傷つけて傷つけられし記憶など時へてひなたの水のやさしさ

「雪降る」より

what is the sky … いま何に怒れる空かと仰ぎみる春降る雪のしたたかな嵩

④　時の点描

「藍色のマグカップ」より

I'm living here … 少しだけ隙間を空けて暮らしゐる心の中の邪気の棲む場所

「はじめの祈り」より

in general … おほかたは一人迷ひてひとり決め悔いも痛みもなべてわがもの

「ともしびの下」より

there are no poems … 子のなきを寂しむ歌のあらぬこと
或る夜夫言ふともしびの下
though I've been living … 意にままに生きて来しかど胸裡に
羽ばたき止まぬ鳥のなほ棲む

「欠けた茶碗」より

once more I realize … 言葉には裏と表のあることを
あらためて知る「また会ひたいね」

「迷路」より

between permitting … 許すこと忘るることのあはひにて
しばし暗き 原野に迷ふ
human life … 人生はいつだつて迷路抽斗の奥に小さな砂漠のありて

「桜桃ほどの」より

my husband says, … 愚痴言はずやさしかつたと過去形に
夫は語れり　わたしの事か

「梅の木の下にて」より

since the day … 拾ひたる猫の名前をプーチンと名付けし日よりロシアは近し

「時の点描」より

the tranquillity ... 安穏はあるいは翼を持たぬこと婚の月日はゆるやかに過ぐ

Kaku Hiroko 賀来　弘子

「アララギ派」歌誌より五十首（2014 年～2016 年)

2014 年

borne on the wind ... 風にのり寺の鐘の音聞こえ来る
ホロホロ紫蘇の花散る夕べ
while I listen ... 政治家の大言壮語を聞きながら二合の米研ぐ福島産米
taking in my hand ... 手に取れど今だ哀しみ迫りきて
表紙を撫でる夫の自分史
'please give me ... もう少し時間を下さい亡き夫の書きし自分史我は開けず
not knowing how ill she was, ... 病む姑のあの苛立ちを汲み取れぬ
病ひ知らずの嫁我なりき
taking a detour ... 父上にと周り道して婿殿が酒買うて来る朧の月夜
smoothly stripping away ... ペラペラと地球のうす皮引き剥し
五月晴れの庭の雑草を引く
in my garden ... 我が庭にトンガのカボチャの花咲けり
去年の冬至のこぼれ種より
in my memory, now, ... 豊後水道に月昇るころ B29 の北上見てゐた今は幻

2015 年

the train departs ... 遠足の園児等さらひて電車発つ
自販機の下より高き虫の音
as I age ... 加齢ゆゑ歯肉の落ちし口元を弔ふやうに口紅を引く
three years ago too ... 三年前もかすかに軋んでゐた治療台に
代替りした歯科医師を待つ
above the chimneys ... 昼の月芒の花穂よりなほ白く廃工場の 煙突にあり
the friend ... 新米を担ぎて訪ね来し友がてんたうむしもつれて来りぬ
the letter I sent my husband ... 嫁ぐ前に夫に送りし我が手紙
仕舞はれてあり姑の文箱に
at the end ... 長時間の検査を終へて瞳孔の開きしままの 帰途の危うし
without waiting ... 瞳孔の収斂待てずに眼科出づ春光我を刺し通すなり
do people pass away, ... 現世での雑念を捨て瞳孔を
開き放ちて人は逝くのか
my mother was the kind of person ... 蝋梅の花の一枝手折りては
客に持たせる母にてありき
a fallen flower, ... 吹かれ過ぎし落花一片舞ひ戻り別れの近き病む夫の背に
that fallen flower ... 夫の背に留まりし落花の一片の押し花のあり我が日記帳
I search ... 古びたる自転車にさす油のやうな
サプリメントなきやコマーシャル見る
when I ask the way ... G パンの膝の破れし青年が道問う我の手を引きくるる

using the Chinese chives ... プランターに芽吹きし韮を褥とし
野良の母猫授乳してをり
no sign of the nursing mother ... 昨夜までの慈母の姿のすでに無し
韮に花咲き雌猫消ゆる
the cicadas' voices ... 蝉の声ハタと止みたり午前十時気温三十度の静寂の町
hearing on the news ...世界一長寿の国とふニュース聞き
決心ついた我家のリフォーム
their teacher, who ... 兵学校に行くなと兄等を諭されし
師は獄中に死に給ひたり

2016年

I, who could never ... いつまでも子離れ出来ぬ我なりき
シリアの母を襟正し見る
saying "take care", ... 「元気で」とテレビレポーターに手を振りて
闇に消えゆく難民一家
leaving behind ... 「先に行くよ」ささやき残し
落ち葉がひらり赤信号を渡って行った
anti-nuclear messages ... 核実験の度に貼られし抗議文原爆資料館
ドームの内壁すき間もあらず
I remember well ... 嫁我に「その優しさが気に入らぬ」
姑なつかしき如月の月明かり
when I pull the thread ... 身の内に深く沈みし思ひ出とふ
糸をたぐれば浮かぶ紅椿
in the rosy sky ... 茜そむ空に精緻なレース編み
広げたやうな蜘蛛の巣のあり
are the cherry blossoms ... 満開の花が誘ふか己が身の
内なる思ひ語り出す友
opening grandfather's diary ... 繙きし祖父の日記に棲みつきし
紙魚（しみ）百五十年の眠りを覚ます
apparently silverfish ... 墨汁は苦手と見えて文字喰まず
その行間に紙魚は息づく
several years ... 幾年も開けたことなき祖父の部屋
よどみの中に 紙魚のうごめく
stories donated ... 郷土資料館へ寄贈の話も立ち消えて
紙魚の天国山積みの古書
in the village house ... 人住まずなりて久しき里の家に
紙魚ひそやかに息づきてをれ
leaving unused ... 「父の日」に送る習ひのオーデコロン
使ひのこして夫旅立てり
beyond love and hate ... 恩讐の彼方に誘ふ風立ちぬ
日米首脳のヒロシマの声
in early summer ... 初夏のヒロシマに来て平和への
道説く首脳等戦争知らず
in Hiroshima ... ヒロシマの風はさやげる青葉若葉
樹木はなべて我より若し
human beings ... 人間は戦と和解を繰り返し
その都度武器は強力となる

I will not forget ... ニョッキリと傾きながらも立ってゐた
原爆ドームを我は忘れじ　（昭和二十七年）
on the small fan ... 手作りの小さな団（うちは）に金魚十匹
それぞれ黒き眼（まなこ）で笑ふ
lured by thunder ... 雷鳴につられて金魚が降って来る
昼寝の夢に生なまとして
each time I wave it ... 扇ぐたび団の金魚の数増えて我の身めぐりに残像泳ぐ

Nagamori Satoshi 長森　總
「寒色暖色」アララギ派叢書第二十一篇
現代短歌社（2013）よりの五十首

フランス　1964–1967

「サクレクールの丘」より

Sacré Coeur ... 照る時は乳色の塔また翳りいま紫のサクレクールの丘

「剥かるる兎」より

when I saunter ... 何気なく階を降り来て隣り家の
庭に兎の剥かるるを見る

「父逝く」より

that day ... ヴォルヴィクの山の泉の溢るるを見つつゐし日に父が逝きしか

「午前十時の灯（あかり）より」

over numerous houseboats ... 夥しき船の家居の上にひびく
降誕祭（ノエル）の鐘は陸の寺より

「抜穴」より

the smell ... 玉葱の香に眼をさされゐる我よ何の為この国に留まりゐる

フランス　1965–1967

「古（いにしへ）の闘士（グラディアタール）」より

I, being accustomed ...青草の上の休息に馴れをりし
我はとまどふスペインの赭（あか）土

「帰国する君」より

what should I, ... 我を励まし我は君のため何を言ふ
君がパリを去るタクシーの中に

日本　1967-1971

「フェルメール」より

from the bottle she holds ... 抱へ持つ瓶より注ぐ牛乳が線となりて
鋭くこの絵を引き締む

フランス　1971-1978

「ペーラシューズ墓地」より

in front of the jet-black ... 黒々と飾りなきドラクロワの墓の前
しづかなる菊の一鉢あり

「ヴェネツィア」より

I buy roast sweet potatoes, ... 焼芋を買ひてヴェネツィアの街をゆく
旅に病む妻が食べるかも知れず

「スイスの旅」より 1973

when I walk the woods... 霧氷の森歩めば霧氷のしづく落つ森白し
空青し今日の降誕祭（ノエル）は

「おお私の人形よ」より

swallows are flying ... 燕ゆきポプラ翻り麦藁は光を返す逢ひたし病む母に

日本　1978-1979

「蛍袋」より

scarlet cloud-trails ... 棚雲の朱映えゐしが消えてゆき
八ヶ岳いま夕べの青さ

「彼方の光」より
treading on the frost ... 我が庭の霜踏みて水を汲みにゆく
流れ来る水と湧きいづる水と

「ナイフの刃」より

for several days ... 兎ゆき雉子の過ぎたる雪の上
幾日きよらにアトリエのめぐり

「立方体の雪」より

the snow exists … 雪はまさに立方体として存在し存在は高田の街を領せり

1986 以後

「ブルゴーニュ再訪」より

in the water are … 並び立つポプラの影は水にあり
描かむと影の乱るるを待つ

「モデルと学生」より 1989

without exception … 例外なき憩ふ形の美しさ休憩時間のモデルに見たり

「アネモネ」より

with the passage of time … 青き夕暮黒き夕闇に移るまで
白き山百合に光はありき

「更紗の紅（くれなゐ）」より

as if discarding … 感覚の濁りを捨つるごとくにも幾度も捨つ筆洗の水

「感覚の震へ」より

just occasionally … この我に稀々に神が贈り来し
色調ありと人には言はず
what was it …求めつつ遂に得ざりしものは何
生まれし時すでに欠けゐしは何

「銀婚の日」より

my wife's heart … わが心向はぬ方へのびのびと向へる妻の心の行方

「地中海の青」より

I rejoice … 生れしより我が持つ色感に調和する南フランスの色を喜ぶ

「ルーブルの恩　パリの恩」より

I ponder … パリの恩われは思へりわが心パリの七年の日々に自立せり

「絶望　希望　絶望」より

the beauty of the colour tone … パレットに作りし色の美しさ
そのままは画布に今日も移らず

「照らし合ふ赤」より

lying dormant ... 体感のうちに潜みて我にあり
十三年フランスに生きし感覚

「鹿の足跡」より

was there a fawn ... 群の中に仔鹿もゐしか森の泉の
水場の泥に足跡がある

「触覚的存在感」より

trying to deepen ... わが観察深めむと己れに集中す
観察が表現に結びつくまで

「妻の視線（一）」より

some days ... 隣室の妻の視線をアトリエに感じる日あり見えぬ視線を

「暖炉」より

seated beside me ... 傍らに火を眺めゐし亡き章子
燃えゐし暖炉燃えゐる暖炉

「短刀の刃先」より

two kinds of shapes: ... 消えてゆく形見えて来る形あり
形の奥に存在がある
it's as if ... パレットに並ぶ絵具のそれぞれに声あるごとし今朝は赤の声

「妻の視線（二）」より

the lemon yellow ... 黄のレモン青みをもちて静かなり
あたたかき向日葵（ひまはり）の黄の下に置けば
the efforts of seeing ... 見る努力考へる努力描く努力
積み上げし努力見せてはならぬ

「寒色のもたらすもの」より

colder, colder – ... もっと寒くもっと寒くと我の絵に
寒色を増やせと今日も皆が言ふ
though I lose my way ... 寒暖の色調の中に迷へども
澄む寒色に心晴れゆく

「描き得ぬもの」より

I was watching clouds ... つぎつぎに生まるる雲を見てゐたり
いかにして描かむ描き得ぬものを

「ホームレス」より

asking for no goods, ... もの乞はず金乞はずなほ生きてゐる
不思議を語れホームレスの誰か

「自由な空」より

in paintings, the sky ... 絵の中で最も自由な筈の空
自由な空が自由に描けぬ

「清しき灰色」より

believing that ... もの言はぬ空間がいつかものを言ふ
時ありと信じ絵をつづけをり

「山荘の冬」より

reddish-yellow needles ... 樺色の針の葉の落葉降りつもり
あたたかに高原の道はふくらむ

「はるかなる赤」

the time has come ... 八ヶ岳すべて赤くなる時は来ぬ
秀づる赤岳が赤を統べつつ

「描きかけの絵」より

can I paint ... 雲の明るさ暗さしづかさはげしさに
動く心を描き得るや我は

「新しき赤」より

I can say ... 絵を描きて成長して来し我なりと言ひ得るはいつかひそかに願ふ
that red ... いま我の見てゐる赤は若き日も見し赤なれど新しき赤
people say ... 壁ひとつ破れと人は言ふといへど見ゆる壁あり見えぬ壁あり
intending ... 鍵穴に遂に合はざる古き鍵捨てむとしつつ幾歳保つ

「黄の大木」より

in a deep-sleep dream ... 尽くるなき赤き絨毯のつづく廊下
歩みゆく歩みゆくレムの夢の中

「ムンクの影」より

is it a human shadow ... 人物の影か黒髪のひろがりか
ムンクの画面の影に脅ゆる

www.ingramcontent.com/pod-product-compliance
Lightning Source LLC
Chambersburg PA
CBHW070938080526
44589CB00013B/1552
9781760416317